Twelve Poems
by Tin Ujević

THE SHEARSMAN CHAPBOOK SERIES, 2013
Martin Anderson *The Lower Reaches*
Richard Berengarten *Imagems 1*
Susan Connolly *The Sun-Artist*
Amy Evans *The Sea Quells*
Alice Kavounas *Thin Ice*
Tin Ujević *Twelve Poems (translated by Richard Berengarten
and Daša Marić)*

Twelve Poems

Dvanaest pjesama

Tin Ujević

Translated from Croatian by
Richard Berengarten and Daša Marić

s hrvatskog preveli
Richard Berengarten i Daša Marić

introduction / uvod
Richard Berengarten

Shearsman Books

First published in English and Croatian
in the United Kingdom in 2013 by
Shearsman Books, 50 Westons Hill Drive, Emersons Green
BRISTOL BS16 7DF

Shearsman Books Ltd Registered Office
30–31 St. James Place, Mangotsfield, Bristol BS16 9JB
(this address not for correspondence)

www.shearsman.com

ISBN 978-1-84861-316-4

Acknowledgements

Thanks to the editors of the following journals and websites, in/on which some
of these translations have appeared: 'Listen how in this perfumed dark', *Celtic
Dawn* (*Yeats Club Review*, "special distinction"), No. 5, 1990; 'Daily Lament',
'Frailty', 'Star on High', and *The Necklace* XXV, XXXI and XXXII, *North Dakota
Quarterly* (*Out of Yugoslavia*, special issue), Winter 1993; 'Blessed morning' and
'Daily Lament', *Borut's Literature Collection*, http://www.borut.com/library/
texts/tin/poetry_u.htm; 'Tonight my forehead gleams', http://www.ezgeetacom/
notturno.html; *The Necklace* XI, XX, XXI ('Nocturne'), XXXII, 'Star on High'
and 'Frailty', *Mediterranean Poetry*: http://www.Mediterranean.nu/?p=1713.

The present selection of translations was first published in the online journal *[sic]*
(no. 3, yr. 2), 2011; and the introduction to this selection is extracted (and slightly
adapted) from an essay which appeared in the same issue, entitled 'A Nimble
Footing on the Coals, Tin Ujević, Lyricist: Some English Perspectives'. http://
www.sicjournal.org/en/contents. Special thanks go to Tomislav Kuzmanović,
the translation editor of *[sic]*, for his valuable critical comments on that essay
and for his support in the preparation of this book, and to Anne Stevenson, for
an improvement in nuance to the translation of *The Necklace* XXI.

Sadržaj / Contents

Tin Ujević, Lyricist

Lelek sebra – izbor
From *Cry of a Slave* (1920)

Kolajna – izbor
From *The Necklace* (1926)

Tin Ujević, Lyricist

The Croatian poet Augustin (Tin) Ujević (1891-1955) is one of the finest Southern Slav lyric poets and one of the great poets of Europe in the first half of the twentieth century. While Tin Ujević's poems are hardly known in English, they are loved in his native Croatia and throughout former Yugoslavia. I say 'loved' advisedly. I don't mean just admired or respected. At least until the break-up of the Yugoslav Federation, many of Tin's lyrics were known by heart and quoted by people all over the country, even those who weren't particularly literary, in much the same way as some of W.B. Yeats's early poems, like 'The Lake Isle of Innisfree', 'He Wishes for the Cloths of Heaven' and 'Down by the Salley Gardens', are known and quoted all over Ireland and the UK. This is mainly because people brought up in the various Yugoslav republics learned some of Tin's poems at school. What is more, the sincerity of affection for him as a poet and as a man is evident even today in South-Slavic countries, especially in the tendency still to refer to him by his pet-name, Tin. And just as the topics of his poems are intimate, and his poetic personality comes across as endearing and sympathetic, so readers in his own language experience and share an intimate response to his poems and feel that they 'know' the 'real' Tin too.

When I first went to live in former Yugoslavia in 1987, the poems of Tin's that I first came across, as might be expected, were his most anthologised pieces. In Split, 1987, Daša Marić asked me to try translating some of these best-known poems, and because my Croatian at that time – or rather, my Serbo-Croat – was a beginner's, she helped me by making literal versions, which we worked from together. Later, in Belgrade and then in Cambridge, I became more or less proficient enough to translate several more poems alone.

Tin's art is delicate, highly crafted, akin to that of filigree. Translation of a poet as intricate as he is sometimes works, sometimes doesn't. You try things out, one after another, you keep your head down, you follow your nose, you fool around, you suddenly wake up in the middle of the night with a better alternative for a phrase running through your head, you turn the light on and scribble it down for fear of forgetting it, you recheck it next morning, you revise, you polish – and sometimes, if you're lucky, one or two poems do come out right.

Of course, I felt it at all times necessary to transmute Tin's *form*, in both the narrow and broad senses. At the micro-level, his patterns of rhyme, rhythm, melopoeia and so on, and at the macro-level, his overall musicality and sense of number, measure and measurement, are integral to his poems and inseparable from their overall meaning – though number and measure of course come in at all other levels too. At any rate, without rendering all these elements, Tin's genius gets lost. 'Meaning' is in no way reducible to 'literal meaning'.

Born in 1891 in Vrgorac, a small town in the Dalmatian hinterland, Tin grew up in Imotski and Makarska, and attended the classical gymnasium in Split. His language and sensibility are indelibly marked by the rugged beauty of the Dalmatian littoral, that narrow, sunbaked, rocky coastline, backed by mountains, facing out over the Adriatic sea and the islands of Hvar, Brač and Korčula. So, for example, in 'Slaboća' ('Frailty'), he writes longingly of "našem plavom, plavom valu,/…našem bijelom, bijelom žalu" (translated as "the waves of our blue blue sea, / and white, white pebbles").

Although Tin's major achievement is as a lyricist, his *oeuvre* is much broader than lyric alone. He was a writer of profound and discerning intellect, broad and capacious interests, inquisitive appetite and eclectic range. His *Collected Works* number sixteen volumes, including poems in many forms, from free verse to the Whitmanesque *verset*, prose-poems, essays, criticism, aphorisms, a book of thoughts and jottings compiled into a personal 'encyclopedia', and translations of fiction, poems and plays by authors as various as Poe, Whitman, Verhaeren, Rimbaud, Gide, Conrad, Meredith and Benvenuto Cellini, among others.

Tin spent many years living in Zagreb, as well as periods in Split, Sarajevo, Mostar, and Belgrade. In his youth, his involvement in the Pan-Slav movement to establish a Yugoslav state earned him the disapprobation of the Austro-Hungarian authorities and the close attention of their police. From 1913 to 1919, he lived in exile in Paris (Montparnasse), where he mingled in the same milieu as other radical writers, artists and intellectuals from Croatia, Bosnia and Serbia, as well as such figures as Picasso, Modigliani, Cocteau, Ehrenburg, and d'Annunzio.

Throughout his life, he lived simply. Well-known as an anarchic bohemian, he was a frequenter of bars and cafés, and always poor. Typical photos show him wearing a battered and ramshackle trilby cocked at a lopsided angle. Affectionate anecdotes about him abound, whether true or apocryphal, like the one I heard about him from poet-friends in Kragujevac, Šumadija, the Serbian heartland. It goes like this: Tin is sitting in a bar with friends, blindfold, tasting wines from all over Yugoslavia and identifying them. He sips half a dozen samples in turn, swirls each one around his mouth, and names all of them in quick succession without a single mistake. Then someone thrusts a glass of water into his hands. He takes a slurp. "No, I don't recognize that one," he says. Other stories aren't so salubrious. There's one about him taking off his hat, picking two fleas out of his hair, and inviting his friends to place bets on a race between them across a café table. Apparently, he spent five years in the French Foreign Legion, though I haven't yet found out when or where he served.

———

Tin's most celebrated lyrics are those in the collection *Kolajna* [*The Necklace*] (1926), the *tour-de-force* 'Svakidašnja jadikovka' ('Daily Lament') as well as several other poems that first appeared with it in *Lelek sebra* [*Cry of a Slave*] (1920). The poems in this small introductory selection are taken from these two books. Tin's poems of the 1920s are immediately approachable in their surface lucidity and simplicity. Every poem is interpretable as a formally composed container or vessel from which an interior feeling emerges. And if it is a truism that exploration and expression of subjectivity are part and parcel of all lyrical poetry, what particularly characterises Tin is that the feeling itself appears to be allowed 'out' and 'up' in the very instant of being felt; or, rather, it is released, simply and clearly, in the precise act of being apprehended. That is to say, it is expressed directly, with neither resistance nor hesitation, and certainly with no need of filtration through the kinds of self-irony, emotional reticence or linguistic gamesmanship that mark a good deal of modernist and postmodernist writing. There is artifice, to be sure, and it is of a high order: Tin is far too sophisticated a poet ever to be interpretable as a naïf. Once (or, rather, if) this point has been accepted, it then becomes evident that his artifice operates so unobtrusively that it *implies* an effortless spontaneity and sincerity. At this level of reading, then, if there is an impression of transparency in Tin's lyrics, this becomes convincing and genuine thanks to his artifice.

—⊷—

The crafted quality of Tin's lyrics is often flawless and their perfection of musicality is comparable, I think, to that of Verlaine. Among all the gems in his 'necklace' of poems, it is fitting, I think, to end these introductory notes by drawing particular attention to the first poem in this selection, 'Daily Lament' ('Svakidašnja jadikovka'). Unrhymed, but with an inescapable, incessant, pounding rhythm, it insists, with slow inevitability, on successive waves of feeling that tumble over one another in rapid succession, oscillating between unease, anxiety, angst, anger, anguish and despair. Here is a poem that, from the point of view of both subject matter and tone, takes every imaginable risk. It is, in all senses, on the edge. At the same time, in its modulation, pace and emphasis, the patterning is flawless. I don't believe there is a human being, however sanguine, who hasn't at some time felt something of what it expresses. What is perhaps most astounding about it is the vitality, vigour and dignity that pulse through it: even in the fullness of its diatribe against life's pains and difficulties, in its beat, its breath, it is paradoxically most full of life. This poem is generally agreed to be Tin's lyrical masterpiece. It is universally powerful.

Richard Berengarten
Cambridge, July 2012

Lelek sebra – izbor (1920)

SVAKIDAŠNJA JADIKOVKA

Kako je teško biti slab,
kako je teško biti sam,
i biti star, a biti mlad!

i biti slab, i nemoćan,
i sam, bez igdje ikoga,
i nemiran, i očajan.

I gaziti po cestama,
i biti gažen u blatu,
bez sjaja zvijezde na nebu.

Bez sjaja zvijezde udesa
što sijaše nad kolijevkom
sa dugama i varkama.

– O Bože, Bože, sjeti se
svih obećanja blistavih
što si ih meni zadao.

– O Bože, Bože, sjeti se
i ljubavi, i pobjede,
i lovora, i darova.

I znaj da Sin tvoj putuje
dolinom svijeta turobnom
po trnju i po kamenju,

od nemila do nedraga,
i noge su mu krvave,
i srce mu je ranjeno.

From *Cry of a Slave* (1920)

DAILY LAMENT

How hard it is not to be strong,
how hard it is to be alone,
and to be old, yet to be young!

and to be weak, and powerless,
alone, with no one anywhere,
dissatisfied, and desperate.

And trudge bleak highways endlessly,
and to be trampled in the mud,
with no star shining in the sky.

Without your star of destiny
to play its twinklings on your crib
with rainbows and false prophecies.

– Oh God, oh God, remember all
the glittering fair promises
with which you have afflicted me.

Oh God, oh God, remember all
the great loves, the great victories,
the wreaths of laurel and the gifts.

And know you have a son who walks
the weary valleys of the world
among sharp thorns, and rocks and stones,

through unkindness and unconcern,
with his feet bloodied under him,
and with his heart an open wound.

I kosti su mu umorne,
i duša mu je žalosna,
i on je sam i zapušten.

I nema sestre ni brata,
i nema oca ni majke,
i nema drage ni druga.

I nema nigdje nikoga
do igle drača u srcu
i plamena na rukama.

I sam i samcat putuje
pod zatvorenom plaveti,
pred zamračenom pučinom,

I komu da se potuži?
Ta njega nitko ne sluša,
ni braća koja lutaju.

O Bože, žeže tvoja riječ
i tijesno joj je u grlu,
i željna je da zapavi.

Ta besjeda je lomača
i dužan sam je viknuti,
ili ću glavnjom planuti.

Pa nek sam krijes na brdima,
pa nek sam dah u plamenu,
kad nisam krik sa krovova!

O Bože, tek da dovrši
pečalno ovo lutanje
pod svodom koji ne čuje.

His bones are full of weariness,
his soul is ill at ease and sad,
and he's neglected and alone,

and sisterless, and brotherless,
and fatherless, and motherless,
with no one dear, and no close friend,

and he has no-one anywhere
except thorn twigs to pierce his heart
and fire blazing from his palms.

Lonely and utterly alone
under the hemmed in vault of blue,
on dark horizons of high seas.

Who can he tell his troubles to
when no-one's there to hear his call,
not even brother wanderers?

Oh God, you sear your burning word
too hugely through this narrow throat
and throttle it inside my cry.

And utterance is a burning stake,
though I must yell it out, I must,
or, like a kindled log, burn out.

Just let me be a bonfire on
a hill, just one breath in the fire,
if not a scream hurled from the roofs.

Oh God, let it be over with,
this miserable wandering
under a vault as deaf as stone.

Jer meni treba moćna riječ,
jer meni treba odgovor,
i ljubav, ili sveta smrt.

Gorak je vijenac pelina,
mračan je kalež otrova,
ja vapim žarki ilinštak.

Jer mi je mučno biti slab,
jer mi je mučno biti sam
(kada bih mogo biti jak.

Kada bih mogo biti drag)
no mučno je, najmučnije
biti već star, a tako mlad!

Because I crave a powerful word,
because I crave an answering voice,
someone to love, or holy death.

For bitter is the wormwood wreath
and deadly dark the poison cup,
so burn me, blazing summer noon.

For I am sick of being weak,
and sick of being all alone
(seeing I could be hale and strong)

and seeing that I could be loved),
but I am sick, sickest of all
to be so old, yet still be young!

SLABOĆA

Po ovoj magli, ovoj kiši –
o pjano srce, ne uzdiši.

Ti ljubilo si uzaludu,
a sada išteš rodnu grudu,

i tvoja čežnja, vapaj roba,
traži odnekud pokoj groba.

– Tu ću skoro da izdahnem,
tu ću skoro da usahnem,

na našem plavom, plavom valu,
na našem bijelom, bijelom žalu;

i sve ću naći što sam trebo
pod tvojim svodom, Sveto Nebo,

plaveti sunca i vedrine
nad zemljom stare domovine.

FRAILTY

In this mist, in this rain –
oh drunken heart, don't drown in pain.

Love unrequited gave no rest,
so now you yearn for earth's breast,

And all your longing, cry of a slave,
is to find some quiet grave:

here my soul will soon expire
and here will wither my desire

on the waves of our blue, blue sea
and white, white pebbles cover me,

and my needs will all come home
under Blessed Heaven's dome,

with sun, calm blue, and clarity,
beneath the ground that once bore me.

Zvijezde u visini

Ne ljubi manje koji mnogo ćuti,
on mnogo traži, i on mnogo sluti,
i svoju ljubav (kao parče kruva
za gladne zube) on brižljivo čuva
za zvijezde u visini,
za srca u daljini.

Ćutanje kaže: u tuđem svijetu
ja sanjam još o cvijetu i sonetu,
i o pitaru povrh svijetle bijede,
i u zar dana i u plavet noći
snim: ja ću doći, ja ću doći.

Stars on High

He loves no less who does not waste his words,
but asks and cares too much, though seeming dumb,
and his whole scope of loving (like a crumb
of bread to feed to hungry teeth), he hoards,
preserving it to give some star on high –
his soul, his heart, his distant destiny.

His silence says: in this world's alien loneliness,
flowers and sonnets occupy my dreams,
with plant-pots perched on seasoned wooden beams –
our poverty's pure, simple lines of loveliness.
beneath the veil of day and night's clean blue,
I'm dreaming: I shall come, I'll come for you.

Kolajna – *izbor* (1926)

I

Stupaj sa svojim mrakom
kroz propast hozrizont;
sa tajnom i oblakom
od fronta, pa do fronta.

Stupaj sa svojom tmušom
kroz ponoć cijele zemlje;
pjevaj sa svojom dušom
gdje god se spava i drijemlje.

V

Ove su riječi crne od dubine,
ove su pjesme zrele i bez buke.
– One su, tako, šiknule iz tmime,
i sada streme ko pružene ruke.

Nisam li pjesnik, ja sam barem patnik
i katkad su mi drage moje rane.
Jer svaki jecaj postati će zlatnik,
a moije suze dati će đerdane.

– No one samo imati će cijenu,
ako ih jednom, u perli i zlatu,
kolajnu vidim slavno obješenu,
ljubljeno dijete, baš o tvome vratu.

FROM THE NECKLACE (1926)

I

Come closer, darkness, lay your hand
across the horizon's wilderness
and cover all of no man's land
with secrecy and cloudiness.

Come closer, dusky haziness
till midnight thickens through the whole
wide world with dreams and drowsiness,
and while it sleeps, sing – from the soul.

V

These words – ripe harvests of black light,
these songs – ripened in silence – reach
cracked and bursting from deep night –
like beggared hands outstretched, beseech –

I'm no poet, but I do know pain –
so I must love my human hurt.
So, from my tears, I'll braid a chain
to ornament a dowry shirt.

– With pearl and coins of minted gold
worth more than any poet wrote –
if only, my beloved child,
you'll wear my necklace at your throat.

XI

Blaženo jutro koje padaš
u svijetlom slapu u tu sobu,
već nema rane da mi zadaš,
počivam mrtav u svom grobu.

Možda ćeš ipak da potpiriš
pepelom iskru zapretanu –
jer evo, trome grudi širiš
čeznućem suncu, jorgovanu.

Dijeliš mi neke tihe slasti
kad o tvom zaru vidim knjige
na polici – i cijeli tmasti
vidik te sobe pune brige.

Za mene ipak nešto fali
u ovoj uzi bez raspeća,
na dragoj usni osmijeh mali,
u čaši vode kita cvijeća.

Blaženo jutro koje padaš
sa snopom svjetla u tu sobu,
već nema smrti da mi zadaš,
no vrati ljubav ovom Jobu.

XI

Blessed morning, you cascade
roaring lightfalls in this room.
How can pain make me afraid,
dead already, in my tomb?

Well, perhaps you can ignite
buried sparks from ash and dust
since the lilac and the light
still swell longing in your breast.

When I lift your veil, you show
lines of quiet, forms of grace
in shelves of books, row on row –
then the whole room's careworn face.

And yet, there's something still I miss
from this crib without a cross,
a smile upon dear lips, the kiss
of flowers in a waterglass.

Blessed morning, while you dress
this room in your translucent robe,
I have no fear of death's caress.
Only give love back to this Job.

XIV

U ovoj gužvi, ovoj stisci
bez oca i bez učitelja
bio sam sam, a moji vrisci,
svi, nose pečat mojih želja.

I svakim slikom, svakim zvukom
dio sam svoje duše dao,
i strijeljao sam lakim lukom,
i gađao sam gdje sam znao.

Izgarah dati nešto Novo
a Bog moj bio moj je Bedem ;
i duh je kriv, i svijetlo Slovo,
ako tek drač i korov jedem.

Najgore tek je u toj stvari,
što evo vidim, monotono:
da umro Duh je – onaj Stari –
a ja sam danas mrtvo Zvono.

XVIII

Osmjejak svaki ljuto plane,
a svaka riječ je kao puška
u naše grudi rastrgane,
u naše srce bez oduška.

Snivamo zelen mir livada
i dom ognjišta u plaveti
i bujno zrnje vinograda
i zrelu tugu mora, ljeti.

XIV

Amid the pressing milling throng
without a guide and fatherless.
I've lived alone and groaned too long:
groans bear my seal of hopefulness.

I hunted every sound and sight,
I gladly parcelled out my soul,
I flexed my bow, my aim was right,
and every shot attained its goal.

I blazed to give out more to all,
with light my letter, God my trust,
and my own spirit criminal
if thorn and bramble were my crust.

But now the dreariest to end
all things is, in this dreary hell,
my spirit's dead – my oldest friend –
and I a cracked and empty bell.

XVIII

Each smile strikes a fresh flare ablaze,
each word, sharp as a gunshot, sounds
into our breasts, torn many ways,
in through our hearts' constricted grounds.

We dream green pastures, where peace shines,
hearthsmoke misting in blue breeze,
clustered grapes strung on their vines,
and deep sad summer-ripened seas.

Plačemo žubor gorskih vrela,
i mahovinu u zabiti,
kad poslije svrhe tužnih djela
čeznemo čiste suze liti.

No, nigdje kraja našem bolu
u bugarenju i uzdahu,
nemir je sličan alkoholu,
a oganj, oganj u mom dahu.

– Osmjejak svaki ljuto plane,
a svaka riječ je kano puška,
u naše suze rastrgane,
u naše srce bez oduška.

XX

U ovom mraku mirisavu
slušajmo kako ječe živci;
i sjećaju na ljutu travu,
a našem grču jesu krivci.

U ovom muku punom boga
zalazi rujna epopeja;
nutrašnja kavga i nesloga
otkriva zelen niz aleja.

Umire naša lijepa tuga,
tuga od svile i baršuna;
varava kao rosna duga,
zlatna i plava kao Luna.

U ovom mraku mirisavu
slušajmo kako ječe živci;
i sjećaju na ljutu travu,
a našem grču jesu krivci.

Each smile strikes a fresh flare ablaze,
each word, sharp as a gunshot, sounds
into our breasts, torn many ways,
in through our hearts' constricted grounds.

We weep whole babbling mountain springs,
for moss of secret haunt and hollow,
and when done with such sorrowings
yearn for cleaner tears to follow.

Our pain is endless, like the wail
of mourners at some village death,
and misery, like alcohol,
sears fire, fire, on my every breath.

XX

Listen how in this perfumed dark
our nerves' thin wires are twanged to flame
as if struck by a nettle's spark.
For wounding us, they'll take the blame.

In this deep hush, with glory filled,
our epic dawn sets, lost from view,
yet vision from this strife is spilled
through the green ranks of the avenue.

The beauty of our grieving frays,
its splendid silk and velvet folds
like dewy rainbows, fade in haze,
fringed like the moon in blues and golds.

Listen how in this perfumed dark
our nerves' thin wires are twanged to flame
as if struck by a nettle's spark.
for wounding us, they'll take the blame.

XXI *Notturno*

Noćas se moje čelo žari,
noćas se moje vjeđe pote;
i moje misli san ozari,
umrijet ću noćas od ljepote.

Duša je strasna u dubini,
Ona je zublja u dnu noći;
Plačimo, plačimo u tišini,
Umrimo, umrimo u samoći.

XXXI

S ranom u tom srcu, tamnu i duboku,
s tajnom u tom trudnu i prokletu biću,
sa zvijezdom na čelu, sa iskrom u oku
gazi stazom varke, mrtvi Ujeviću;

smrt je tvoja ljubav pri svakome kroku,
smrt je u tvom iću, u tvojemu piću,
smrt je u tvom dahu, i u tvojem boku,
smrt, i smrt, i smrt u Nadi i Otkriću.

Što ti vrijedi polet u vlastitu čudu,
što ti vrijedi volja i voljenje slijepo?
Srce bije, pluće diše uzaludu;

gle, bez fajde ljubiš sve dobro i lijepo;
kao sveli miris u razbitu sudu
pogiba u tebi pjev što si ga tepo.

XXI *Nocturne*

Tonight, my forehead gleams
with sweat that bathes each eye;
my thoughts blaze through dreams,
tonight, of beauty I shall die.

The soul's core is passion deep
in night's abyss, a blazing cone.
Hush, weep in silence. Let us weep
and let us die. We'll die alone.

XXXI

Deep in that heart, black wounds he dare not show;
he's weary, cursed, a being in distress,
that sparkle in the eyes, that starry brow –
you're dead, Tin. All your paths are emptiness.

Death is your love, in every step you take,
death, in your belly and in every breath,
death is your drink and daily bread you break,
in expectation and attainment, death.

What use blind love or hope without a goal,
what use desire's wild dash, when there's no cure
through breathing lungs or heartbeats, for the soul,

and though your loves are beautiful and pure
like faded perfume in a broken bowl,
none of your babbling larksong can endure?

XXXII

Ponore! more povrh moje glave
i zlatne ribe danom od kristala,
ja pitam gdje je Mjesečina pala
i gdje se gorski horizonti plave.

Zora je puna nježne jasne strave,
a miso je – bistra, ledna – stala;
ne zanima me skala, ni spirala,
ni česti odraz uzdrmane jave.

Srce je svijeta plodno i duboko
a čovjek slomljen pod težinom neba
a život krila visoko – visoko.

Nebrigo žene, presitosti hljeba,
od ritma misli zadnja spona puca
A srce kuca, bilo kuca, kuca.

XXXII

The Gulf! Whole oceans scaled over my head,
and gold fish fashioned out of crystallites,
I ask where Madam Moonlight's lain abed,
and blue horizons haze blue mountain heights.

The dawn is spiked with delicate clear dread,
thought's needles – piercing, lucid – snap and freeze.
No scales or spirals raise me, spirited,
nor mirrorings of rocked realities.

The heart's a world unfathomed, fertile, deep,
and man, beneath his lead sky, breaks and sinks,
while life, a seagull, soars above his head.

Aye, well-fed easy woman, stuffed on bread,
thought's rhythms broke our last connecting links,
but oh, how heart and pulse beat, beat and leap.

Richard Berengarten: Bibliography

Selected Writings, Shearsman edition

Vol. 1   *For the Living : Selected Longer Poems, 1965–2000*
Vol. 2   *The Manager*
Vol. 3   *The Blue Butterfly*   *(The Balkan Trilogy, Part 1)*
Vol. 4   *In a Time of Drought*   *(The Balkan Trilogy, Part 2)*
Vol. 5   *Under Balkan Light*   *(The Balkan Trilogy, Part 3)*

Poetry

The Easter Rising 1967
The Return of Lazarus
Double Flute
Avebury
Inhabitable Space
Angels
Some Poems, Illuminated by Frances Richards
Learning to Talk
Tree
Roots/Routes
Black Light
Croft Woods
Against Perfection
Book With No Back Cover
Manual : the first 20
Holding the Darkness (*Manual: the second 20*)
Holding the Sea (*Manual: the third 20)*
Manual: the fourth 20

As Editor

An Octave for Octavio Paz
Ceri Richards : Drawings to Poems by Dylan Thomas
Rivers of Life
In Visible Ink : Selected Poems, Roberto Sanesi 1955-1979
Homage to Mandelstam
Out of Yugoslavia
For Angus
The Perfect Order: Selected Poems, Nasos Vayenas, 1974-2010

www.ingramcontent.com/pod-product-compliance
Lightning Source LLC
Chambersburg PA
CBHW021948040426
42448CB00008B/1291